embracing disruption
a cloud revolution manifesto

Nathan Toups

Brad Carleton

Version 1.1

ISBN: 1489593349
ISBN-13: 978-1489593344

DEDICATION

This manifesto is dedicated in memory of Aaron Swartz for his contributions to Internet Freedom and Open Access. In his honor, 50% of all profits from this manifesto will go towards organizations that fight to protect our basic online rights and freedoms.

CONTENTS

ACKNOWLEDGMENTS

This manifesto was funded through Kickstarter, the world's largest funding platform for creative projects.

None of this would have been possible without our amazing backers on Kickstarter. We thank all of you. Below are some of our largest contributors listed by backing-level.

Platinum
- Elizabeth Christian & Associates Public Relations
- Gary and Dinah Toups

Gold
- Kristy Sprott - The Format Group | formatllc.com
- Edwin & Regina Walker - Family Health of Louisiana
- Javo Villalobos

Silver
- Steve Guengerich Appconomist: Your Guide to the Global App Economy (follow us @Appconomist)
- Zack Williams (@zdw), Artisan Computer (http://artisancomputer.com)
- Barbara S. Walker - Livingston Parish Children's Choirs www.LPCCsing.org
- Mike Braeuer - Explore Austin
- Gary Larizza - @glarizza
- Walter and Debbi Mitchell
- Danny and Karen Burnett

AUTHORS

Brad Carleton | author | @techpines
Brad started Tech Pines, a javascript and cloud consulting company in 2010, pioneering in javascript development both on the browser and on the server. Prior to starting his own company, he worked in the hustle and bustle of the Austin tech industry. As an entrepreneur with a passion for development and the open source community, he participates in projects like CTX Givecamp to help non-profits with improvements to existing web technologies.

Nathan Toups | author | @rojoroboto
Nathan is a professional geek with a background in collaborative design. He honed his professional technology skills after college and now owns and operates rojoroboto, a boutique technology consulting firm in Austin, TX. He is an expert in mobile device and cloud integration in the workplace, specifically with Mac OS X, iOS, and the cloud. He has spoken at SXSW and MacTech Conference and he writes for technical journals such as MacTech Magazine.

EDITOR & ILLUSTRATOR

Martin Whitmore | illustrator | @MartinWhitmore
Martin is an artist & illustrator living in Austin, TX.
When he's not drawing zombies and pinup girls, he
loves helping small businesses and solo entrepreneurs
get their message across with striking illustrated
promotions. He has illustrated numerous published
books and eBooks, and works with Megan Elizabeth
Morris as the artist half of Ideaschema -
www.ideaschema.com. You can also see more of his
work on his personal site, www.martinwhitmore.com.

Susan Butler | editor | @clevrcat
Susan is a freelance editor and Mac-based IT nerd
with a background in small enterprise and boutique
craft making. Her consulting business, ClevrCat, is the
front for her editing and digital media curation
ventures. She has a passion for learning and
encouraging technological empowerment in women,
and is fluent in both English and Feline. In her free
time she can be found making custom bow ties for
her second company, Finley Park.

THE MANIFESTO

We are the embracers of disruption.
We are the pioneers of a new frontier.

We are the denizens of a new world built by human minds and machines.
Our world grows stronger, faster, and more capable every day.

We embrace:

- Bold visions of the future backed by real data.
- Distributed systems with no central authority.
- Freedom to share information and self express.
- Strength through a global community of hackers and free-thinkers.

We value:

1. Expression over conformity.
2. Standards over servitude.
3. Distribution over centralization.
4. Reuse over waste.
5. Data over dogma.

This is our cloud revolution manifesto.

PART 1: INTRO

Congrats on Your Cloud Baby

The story of this book starts with two guys at a bar and the idea that there wasn't an accessible, easy-to-read book about the cloud and the technological revolution engulfing the planet.

Having never published a book before, and not having much in the way of money, we decided to reach out to the rest of the world for help. We signed up for a web service called Kickstarter and asked anyone who thought it was a cool idea to donate.

They actually have a term for this process called crowdfunding. Our one little idea was able to bounce all around the internet, and people who found it interesting threw a little money our way to make it a reality.

Thanks to a bunch of generous donors we got this book funded, which meant that we got the funds to pay for an editor and an illustrator.

That's pretty cool. We didn't need a big fancy publishing company to give us an advance to write the book. We didn't need to tirelessly ship our drafts out in hopes of being chosen. We reached out to the community at large and they came to our rescue.

But how do you distribute a book? You might think you need printing presses to make the book, big trucks to move the book and storefronts to sell the book. However, we decided to let the internet be our distributor.

So now, anyone with an internet connection anywhere in the world can read this book for free.

That is what the cloud is all about.

It's a reimagining of the internet. It's about people connecting with people and doing amazing things. It's about possibilities and the future. It's about individuals and ideas. It's about you.

PART 2: MONEY

This Series of Tubes Has Money in It

They want to deliver vast amounts of information over the Internet. And again, the Internet is not something that you just dump something on. It's not a big truck. It's a series of tubes. - Senator Ted Stevens

If Ted Stevens is right, and this vast network of computers around the world is just a series of tubes, then there is one unmistakable truth: there is a lot of money in those tubes.

It's estimated that the combined economic output of the internet is greater than the energy, mining and agriculture sectors put together. Perhaps surprisingly, most of that economic power is derived not from the big tech companies like Google, Apple or Amazon. Instead, it's the economic power of traditional businesses that are reaching beyond their potential to make the cloud such a potent force in the world economy.

It's restaurants and shops that have new and exciting ways of interacting with their clients through social media. It's small businesses that can now do their accounting, invoicing and payroll online for a small monthly fee. It's drug companies that can run a 50,000 core cloud-based supercomputer to search for new drugs to fight cancer.

The cloud has become not just a source of wealth and innovation, but it is also the place where an enormous number of the world's financial transactions actually take place. You have ATM machines dialing up to check account balances and high frequency trading algorithms making millisecond stock trades.

In a way, it all makes sense. Think of the taco truck vendor who is now able to swipe your credit card on his phone. It's just simpler. It's easy to understand how vendors like Gap, Target or Zappos impact the internet. It's less obvious when it's a taco stand in an Airstream trailer that is transforming the way we do business. At the end of the day, money is just information. (Whether in legal tender or digital form.)

And if money brings power, then power brings the chance to transform the world.

A CLOUD REVOLUTION MANIFESTO

In Bitcoin We Trust

At the dawn of civilization money didn't exist. Instead, people bartered for the things they wanted. Bartering is great in some ways but it also has its limitations. How many clay jars equal a goat? How many spearheads equal a hut? Those were some tricky questions for early man so society decided it was better to have one standard for exchange. They decided that they needed money.

While some early cultures dabbled with using shells and strings, precious metals entered the picture as the obvious candidate for money. Precious metals are rare and shiny. Perfect for trade and stamping your rulers face on.

Unfortunately, the system of basing money on precious metals, gold and silver specifically, came to a crashing halt in the 1970s. The US government decided that the dollar would no longer be backed by gold, but instead, by trust. In fact, the slogan on paper money, "In God We Trust," took on even greater meaning after the switch. Now, your faith in those little green pieces of paper were tied up in your faith in government.

This is all fine and good. Governments across the world, bastions of centralized power, have taken the reigns; they get to decide what money is and everyone just needs to accept it.

There is one little rub in this whole story. The cloud has created its first digital currency. Out of the ether a currency called Bitcoin has started trading across the internet.

As of this writing, there is over 300 million dollars in Bitcoins and in the last 24 hours 1.7 billion dollars in trades have taken place.

What is this currency based on? Trust in a precious metal? Trust in a government? Nope, it's based on something that is actually much easier to trust: Math.

Based on a few complex crypto-algorithms the concept of a decentralized cloud currency, with no ties to any central bank, was born.

Amazon's Revolution by Evolution

Amazon.com is a behemoth built on a foundation of incremental improvement and change. Many people know it is the world's largest online retailer. But what far fewer people know is that Amazon.com is one of the leading innovators in cloud technology.

A special division of the company known as Amazon Web Services (AWS) has built a collection of low-cost cloud-based services that allow other companies to rent servers, storage and other computing services by the hour. Amazon uses a technology which allows them to host multiple "virtual servers" on special hardware. With a click of a button companies can create and terminate these servers in a matter of seconds. Companies only pay for what they use and there are no upfront setup fees. This allows small companies to avoid the high cost of investing thousands of dollars in equipment and it empowers large companies with the flexibility to react to customer demand.

Thousands of companies rely on AWS everyday. - Netflix, the online streaming service, has built their entire cloud infrastructure on top of Amazon's cloud.

- Social networking giant Pinterest has been able to quickly scale from less than 10,000 users in 2010 to more than 48 million users in February of 2013.

- Cloud-based file syncing service Dropbox uses Amazon's low cost cloud storage to reliably house user data.

- Obama for America (OFA) built more than 200 applications for President Obama's 2012 reelection campaign.

- NASA's Jet Propulsion Laboratory leveraged AWS to meet demands of live stream images and video from the 2012 landing of Curiosity on Mars.

- And the list goes on...

The most exciting aspect of Amazon Web Services isn't the service itself, it is the philosophy and leadership that drives it.

In 2012, Dr. Werner Vogels, chief technology officer of Amazon.com and one of the chief architects of AWS, outlined the core philosophy of AWS at the first-ever AWS re:Invent Technology Conference in Las Vegas. In his keynote speech he introduced the notion of "hypothesis-driven development." That is, the cloud makes it easy and inexpensive to test out new ideas. Instead of relying on old (and expensive) ways of thinking your company can push the boundary of understanding with a feedback-loop of small changes and measuring results of those changes. In fact, the core philosophy of "hypothesis-driven development" is what has built Amazon's cloud from the ground up.

Back in 2004 an engineer at Amazon proposed

that Amazon.com could profit from reselling underutilized server resources to the public. Fast forward to today and Amazon has built more than 34 cloud infrastructure services for themselves and continued to offer these additional resources to the public. Every month Amazon is either introducing new services or lowering costs to customers for those services. In any given month, Amazon's services don't really have any dramatic changes but if you look back over the last nine years Amazon's cloud offerings have radically shifted.

There are companies now that adopt these revolutionary new tools to reduce the time to market, build testing grounds for innovation and rapidly scale their services to meet growing demand. None of which would have been possible 10 years ago at the low cost of entry like today.

In conclusion, Amazon Web Services and the philosophy that drives it is giant and far-reaching. While few people outside of the technology world have noticed, AWS has diligently and incrementally built a cloud empire. This empire has shifted our way of thinking about information, the internet and the cloud. The revolutionary philosophy that they have introduced and the data-driven nature of their incremental and evolutionary change is now embedded into the fabric of cloud-dwelling humankind.

PART 3: SOCIAL

Making Losers Cool Since '93

Sometimes people wonder what the difference is between the internet and the web. Often you hear the two terms used interchangeably or munged together into an endearing term like "interwebs."

So what's the difference?

Well, the internet is old. It's been around since the late 60s and it's just not that cool. It's what your traditional nerd would have appreciated. Machines talking to each other in unintelligible 1's and 0's all over a vast global network...

Fast track to 1993 and something cool did happen. A lowly techie working for CERN (best known for particle accelerators and atom smashing) did something pretty novel.

He created this idea of the web, a way for real live people to interact over the internet through a simple web browser installed on their computers.

Originally the web was built so that scientists could share documents and research with one another. However, it wasn't long before non-scientists started getting into the game and you had the tech explosion of the 90s.

You had quirky startups like Google with their one little search box who would eventually become one of the titans of global innovation and progress. You had ambitious entrepreneurs trying to take their crazy ideas into the Fortune 500. Some like Amazon succeeded mightily while many others like Pets.com would be relegated to the trash bin of history.

But more important than the ramifications for businesses was the impact that the web had on normal people.

Finally, instead of just connecting machines to machines, we had built a system that really let people connect with people.

The whole paradigm had changed. You could actually have meaningful relationships with individuals, groups or organizations no matter where they were physically located. You could have an identity as a person online. You could be cool even if in your hometown you weren't.

Now, instead of losing our humanity in a sea of 1's and 0's, we are able to express our creativity and individuality beyond what was ever thought possible. From the early days of AOL and Geocities to the massive social networks of Facebook and Twitter, the cloud is allowing us to be greater than the sum of our parts.

But if we don't protect it, we could lose everything.

A CLOUD REVOLUTION MANIFESTO

Amplifying Obsession

Check in. Play another round. Compare your status with your friends. Like that post. Tag your friends. Comment on that article. Get in a comment debate. Check in. Check the weather. See what is on the news. Share that article. Like that post. Update your feed. Accept that friend request. Google yourself. Look up who that actor was on season three of that show. Check your email. Check your likes. Check the trends of that hashtag you were following. Check in. Post that picture. Tag your friends. Like. Like. Like. Scan. Share. Post. Check in. Like. Post. Like. Scan. Accept. Share. Like.

Seth Godin calls this the fear of missing out. Unchecked, it is the most powerful driving force behind modern social networks. We have always had it but now we have the means to amplify it so loudly that it fuels our obsessions.

Social Media for Dictators

There are technology revolutions and then there are revolution revolutions. And if you were a dictator during the Arab spring, then you probably felt the full force and fury of both.

In 2010, the people of the Arab world decided that enough was enough. Tired of government oppression, tired of lackluster economic opportunity and tired of being too afraid to do anything about it. Ordinary people started to get involved.

Before the Arab Spring, many uprisings in the Middle East simply ended in bloodshed and repression. What could possibly be different this time? How could the powerless topple the powerful?

Revolutions aren't built on guns and soldiers, they are built on ideas and people. And the new social media platforms offered a way to disseminate and collaborate on those ideas like never before. The revolution would be digitized!

Nowhere was this more evident than in Egypt, the heart of the Arab world. Using Facebook, Twitter, Flickr, blogs and any other online tool at their disposal, citizen journalists and activists were able to organize huge protests across the country. The foundations of their revolution were born in the heated discussions of simple Facebook forums. As one Egyptian activist put it, "We use Facebook to schedule the protests, Twitter to coordinate, and YouTube to tell the world."

The old regime never stood a chance. Finally, after decades of dictatorship, it collapsed with the help of a new generation of thinkers and activists empowered by the cloud.

PART 4: GOVERNMENT

Drones and iPhones

In August 2012, Apple rejected an app named Drones+ for being "objectionable and crude." What is troubling about this was that this was the third rejection for this app. Each time that Josh Begley submitted his app to the App Store, Apple rejected it for a different reason. The first time was for being "not useful." The second time it was rejected was for containing a corporate logo (which was promptly removed).

Josh's app was simple. It listed all reported drone strikes. You could view them in a list or on a map. It also had the ability to use push notifications to notify you of newly reported drone strikes. It is built on top of publicly available information and didn't include any sort of grotesque imagery. His goal was to raise awareness of the largely secretive robotic strikes happening in the Middle East.

The iPhone and smartphones like it have revolutionized how people interact with the cloud, but there is a lurking question related to what can and cannot be loaded on these devices. As of this writing, Apple tightly controls app distribution through its App Store. It follows a philosophy known as "the walled garden" approach or a "closed ecosystem." This means that any software (app) that runs on the iPhone must be approved by Apple first. Primarily, this is to protect the average iPhone user from buggy software, spyware and viruses. This is also a breeding ground for Apple to censor what is available to the iPhone user. For instance, Apple decides what is and is not appropriate. Apple decides what qualifies as pornography. Apple reserves the right to reject applications that "duplicate functionality."

Even today, if you search for "drone" on the iPhone there are several dozen drone-simulator games, but when it comes to Drones+ it is nowhere to be found. Oddly enough, some of the drone apps are violent games. When Apple decides to block the self expression of an app developer that is aggregating data publicly available on the web, but they allow the violent fantasy of a drone game in their app store, red flags should be raised.

By attempting to block a political statement Apple is making an even more ominous political statement. Instead of building an open and transparent platform to publish apps, Apple uses a curated "walled garden" where reasons behind accepting and rejecting apps can be arbitrary and politically motivated. This is the danger of having a company exclusively curate what is allowed to run on your devices. What Apple has built in the name of safety, simplicity and security lends itself to tyrannical manipulation of self expression.

A CLOUD REVOLUTION MANIFESTO

Big Brother is Watching

Governments around the world have an uneasy relationship with the cloud. At first it seemed like a wonderful platform for economic growth and enhanced communication. However, there is one little snag. The cloud is decentralizing. It brings power to the people. This can have the unintended consequence of making the G-men of the world a little twitchy.

Nowhere is this more evident than in China where paranoia in the top ranks of government has led to a sustained and continuous assault on internet freedoms.

In June of 1989, a bloody crackdown of pro-democracy protests in China's Tiananmen Square left thousands dead and democracy for the Chinese people crushed.

A mere twenty years later a different kind of crackdown would take place.

According to the South China Morning Post, Chinese censors released a statement saying, "In order to improve the internet content and provide a healthy environment for our netizens, we have designated 3 to 6 June as the national server maintenance day. This move is widely supported by the public."

Turns out that "national server maintenance day"

and the anniversary of the Tiananmen Square massacre are the same. The day that the Chinese government needs to run repairs and take everyone offline just so happens to coincide exactly with a twenty year old massacre in the capital.

Can the Chinese government really take the internet down for repairs to cover up its past mistakes? Can they get away with stifling the innovation and creativity of its people?

And what if you're like me, a citizen of the United States of America? Surely a free and open society like the US isn't paranoid and scared of its own people.

If you agree, you would be wrong.

There are plenty of reasons for Uncle Sam to be paranoid these days. There are terrorists, online sexual predators and that "Wikileaks guy."

The US government has more or less decided that in the interest of national security, and with the help of the Patriot Act, that they can spy on us as they wish. Our online privacy and our fourth amendment constitutional right to privacy are not being respected.

The threat from government oppression and central authorities won't ever go away but neither should our collective resolve to stand up to them.

Obama's Cloud Beat Romney's Servers

In 2012, the presidential election wasn't only between a Republican and a Democrat, it was an election between an old and new way of thinking about technology on the campaign trail. These campaigns differed greatly in how they built their voter databases, designed tools for volunteers and even how they funded their technology operations.

Democratic incumbent President Barack Obama took an aggressively cloud-focused approach. Not only did he under spend the Romney campaign by $14.5 million on technology, he hired a team of very talented web developers and cloud experts who built a sophisticated voter database codenamed Narwhal. Narwhal was built in-house, based on free and open source software. On top of this database they built applications that volunteers could use on the front lines of the campaign. Two of the biggest applications were Dashboard and Call Tool. Dashboard allowed volunteers to organize into groups, communicate through message boards, view upcoming events and more. Call Tool empowered volunteers to make and track phone calls on behalf of the campaign.

Not only were the Obama campaign efforts focused and functional, they ran their entire campaign without buying physical servers to run Narwhal or their web applications. This was only possible using the latest cloud technologies like Amazon Web Services.

Republican nominee Mitt Romney stuck with a more traditional mix of high-priced information technology (IT) consultants, expensive enterprise Microsoft solutions and commercial software solutions purchased from close friends to the campaign. In reaction to the Obama campaign's Narwhal database, they built their own database codenamed Orca (the Narwhal's natural enemy). Orca was built on Microsoft database technology, and instead of being hosted in the cloud, it was housed in a data center in the Northeast.

Not only were the campaigns radically different in their structure, they differed greatly in their discipline and preparedness as well. While Narwhal was an integral part of the Obama campaign for months, Orca wasn't fully operational until 6 a.m. on Election Day. Narwhal and all related applications had an advanced testing and deployment scheme while Orca had never been properly stress tested for "real world" activity before it went live on the day of the election. Instructions for Dashboard and Call Tool were simple and straightforward while Orca shipped with a 60 page PDF manual the day before the application went live. On Election Day, Obama's servers were running smooth and reliably while Romney's servers were plagued with crashing, invalid passwords and configuration mishaps.

In the end, Obama's campaign won in a clean sweep when it came to technology. Not only were they better organized and more prepared, but the Obama campaign embraced the disruptive technology and forward thinking innovators that empowered his campaign to take full advantage of the cloud. Romney was defeated and left with old technology ideas and broken promises from his vendors.

PART 5: SECURITY

Tinfoil Hats

Imagine the life of a telemarketer. Eight hours a day, five days a week, everything he does and says is tracked for performance metrics. He is measured on promptness, courteousness, speed, friendliness, articulation, call length, customer satisfaction, calls per hour, volume of sales closed, sales per call closed, up-sales as a percentage of sales, and a myriad of other performance metrics. To take things further, when he is in the office calls are monitored for quality controls and his browsing history on his computer is tracked to ensure that he is maximizing productivity while he is in the office (not to mention that they block time wasting sites like Facebook and Twitter).

For 40 hours a week he is a machine. He is good at his job. He hits his numbers. He can close deals. Several months a year he is even employee of the month. His boss finds him to be self-motivated, a team player and a quick learner. He is part of the new employee training team. Mr. Telemarketer is a model employee.

As long as the values of Mr. Telemarketer and Mr. Boss are in sync, life is great. But what happens if they get out of sync? Or what happens if his company oversteps their boundaries?

Have you ever had a job in which you knew you were being watched? Imagine you have just started a new job as that telemarketer. You are being trained on using the phones. Your boss tells you and the customer that your phone calls will be recorded for training purposes. Not only are you thinking about working with the customer but you are also busy thinking about how you sound to your boss while you are taking the phone call.

Until you are acclimated to how things work around the office, and you have adjusted to exactly what is expected of you, your behavior will be awkward. You will be so busy worrying about messing up that you might stutter, pause and second guess your actions. All things you don't want to do in front of your new boss.

Early on, your boss listens to every phone call and critiques you. At first you are apprehensive, but as time goes on, you improve. Eventually your boss only listens to your calls at random.

It doesn't matter though. The possibility that your boss could be listening to your phone conversation still exists and that affects your behavior. Because you have no way of knowing which phone calls your boss might be listening to, you must treat every phone call as if your boss were listening to you. On each call, in the back of your mind, you acknowledge that your boss could be right there on the line listening to everything you have to say.

So what? In most jobs this is expected. What's the big deal? Simple. We behave differently when we think we are being monitored. Instead of behaving how you want to naturally behave, you add an extra step. Unless you are confident that your natural behaviors are always in accordance with the constraints of what is deemed acceptable, you behave how you think the person watching you wants you to behave.

Why does the boss monitor your phone calls? Your boss probably wants you to do a good job. Your boss may even have a set of guidelines on acceptable behavior handed down from an even higher department in the company. Doing a good job probably means conforming to how she wants things done. Monitoring your behavior allows your boss to ensure that you act in accordance with her values and the values of the company. If you value your job, you will conform to behaving in a way in which your boss deems acceptable. If you latch on to the company culture, you might even become the next Mr. Telemarketer.

This might be easy if your values naturally align with those of your boss, but if they do not, you could get reprimanded or fired.

So, to keep your job, you operate within the expectations of the position. If you stay within the acceptable range, life is good. It is even possible that if you like the company and you are rewarded well, the small natural differences you have with the company are realigned in your attitude. You might even change your values to align with the company so that compliance is effortless and even fun.

But even in the most liberal jobs with the most pleasant of work environments, if you are monitored and surveilled, there is something inherently asymmetric with your relationship. Your boss holds a substantial amount of information about you, and you hold a relatively small amount of information about him. When your job is going well and everything is rosy, this isn't a perceivable issue. But if things go sour, your employer has the upper hand.

For instance, back in 2009 the Wall Street Journal reported that Google had built an algorithm that could predict which of their employees was most likely to quit, sometimes even before the employee themselves were aware of it. You can only imagine the odd feeling that Google employees must have had after reading that article. Google might be able to predict if they were going to quit, but Google employees had no means to predict if they were going to get fired. This is precisely information asymmetry in the workplace.

Or, for example, in 2011 a man complained to a Target store that his high school daughter was receiving advertisements for maternity clothing only to find out later that she was indeed pregnant. Target is able to use customers' purchasing history to predict a woman's "pregnancy prediction score." Target accomplished this by analyzing the purchasing history of women in various stages of pregnancy and they were able to find reliable indicators. Target used this "pregnancy score" for targeted marketing campaigns. This predictor is so reliable and so early at detecting matches that Target suspected that the man's daughter was pregnant before he did.

Whether you realize it or not your behavior is being monitored online. Data about you is being gathered every day. It is saved into databases, aggregated with other people's data and analyzed.

This isn't a nefarious conspiracy theory; it is the reality of the Google-powered, Facebook-integrated, post-9/11 Patriot Act world in which we live. Now let's put on our tin foil hats boys and girls, it's about to be a bumpy ride.

Admittedly, an overwhelming majority of us in the US are like Mr. Telemarketer. We live our lives in such a way that we don't clash with the boss, or in this case, the government. But unlike Mr. Telemarketer, we can't just quit our job or be fired if we don't like what is going on. We aren't dealing with a job here, we are dealing with our lives.

A byproduct of an increasingly connected world

in which we are always carrying a smart phone, always logged in to our email and always logged into our social media accounts, is that it makes it easier than ever to have our behavior monitored and surveilled. We have an asymmetric relationship with those in positions of power and they have the information advantage. They are able to build a clear picture of us but we aren't able to build a clear picture of them (or even know if we are being monitored).

So why are we concerned? Privacy and the risk of losing privacy aren't things to worry about when times are peaceful and when your life is going well. But, if the tools are in place for such monitoring to be abused, eventually it will be. If leadership happens to take a turn for the worse or you happen to be associated with a group of people who are considered dangerous, high risk, or enemies, your entire life could turn upside down in a matter of days.

This might be hard for many of us to imagine in the United States, but for some nations around the world this is not so far fetched. Two examples in recent history are the Arab Spring and the Great Firewall of China.

On January 27, 2011, the Egyptian government cut 80,000,000 citizens off from the internet almost instantly. The government, in conjunction with all private internet service providers (some of which were owned by international corporations headquartered in the US), disabled internet access to the outside world. Soon, it became a cat and mouse game between rebels and the establishment on reactivating communication with the rest of the world.

With the help from anonymity and anti-censorship software such as The Onion Router (TOR) and dedicated help from thousands of hackers around the world, Egyptian rebels were able to regain internet access and share with the world what was truly going on in their country.

In China, censorship, monitoring and web traffic blocking have become widespread. Not only are services like Twitter and Google blocked in China, more recently China increased their control over the behavior of citizens by blocking or hijacking secure and encrypted forms of communication to those outside the country.

If it is possible that such monitoring tools could be abused, it is sensible to assume that they are going to be abused.

More simply, if there is a possibility that you are being monitored online, the only sensible behavior would be to act as though you are being monitored online.

Put into the context of the cloud and there are

some important questions that arise.

- How do we know we are secure in the cloud?
- How do we know who to trust in the cloud?
- How do we know who is monitoring us in the cloud?
- Who are we to trust in the cloud? Especially when we know that it increases our risk of exposure to information asymmetry.

In the internet and in the cloud, trust is the key subject. Most of us pay for access to services such as email and file storage in which we are incapable of truly understanding the underlying technology. When we pay for these services we enter trust-based relationships with the service providers to properly maintain the data, protect our privacy and to continue to operate in a manner that makes our lives easier. For most of us, being surveilled is the last thing on our minds. If a government snooped around my Dropbox or Gmail account it would be pretty boring stuff.

In existing law in the United States, our federal government has the ability to request records from any service online. The ability to request records is nothing new but what is unique to our post-9/11 world is that our federal government now has the ability to request records in secret. They can request records from a service provider like Gmail with a special gag order that forbids Google from notifying anyone that records were ever requested.

Select agencies in the federal government now have the ability to request, record and compile vast amounts of data without notifying anyone that such records were ever requested. This is largely performed in the name of counter terrorism. With poor oversight and few details on what is being requested and how frequently, such a program is begging to be exploited and abused.

The funny thing about surveillance, though, is that it doesn't matter if you are actually being surveilled or not. If the possibility exists, you behave as if you are being surveilled. If you feel your conversation could be monitored, it affects the way you express yourself with others, even in the relative privacy of direct conversation.

But let's take a step back for a second. Let's step away from the tin foil hat worries of government monitoring. Let's look at how existing technologies could be abused.

Our final topic for our tinfoil hat is a doozy: Encryption.

Encryption technologies, like the kind that is used to securely access your banking online, are quite mature, technically. If you use a modern web browser and the website you are connecting to uses modern encryption, the odds of someone "snooping" on your conversation is almost zero. Well, that would be true if we were 100% certain of the authenticity of your banking website.

When you access your banking website on a modern web browser, you will probably see a large green bar or a secure-looking padlock that indicates that your connection to your bank is secure and trusted.

Sadly, it isn't that simple. The same protection and care that goes into making that little padlock green is also the weakest link. It all boils down to trust.

On your computer, you have a set of "root authorities." These are organizations that your computer, browser and banking website have agreed are trustworthy enough to entrust your encryption. This relatively small set of trustworthy authorities are assumed and trusted not to make a mistake, not to cooperate with foreign governments for espionage and not to be operated by organized crime. This trust was made early on and this trust is forever.

Problems with the existing model reach far and wide. In the past, security researchers have found ways to trick the browser into thinking a site was properly secured. Famously one certificate authority issued false certificates for Google, Yahoo and Microsoft, allowing hackers to "spoof" legitimate websites and possibly steal sensitive data.

These certificate authorities give us a false sense of security. Why should we be forced to trust a small number of companies with our encryption when we could build a much more reliable system based on "distributed trust?"

Instead of having a single authority confirm the validity of my secured connection, why don't we build a system in which a group of trusted authorities reach a consensus? This way, if any one authority was compromised, the system wouldn't fail. This alternate model for validating certificates by consensus was originally developed by the Perspectives Project at Carnegie Mellon University and later implemented in proof-of-concept by Moxie Marlinspike called Convergence.io.

Distributed systems are the key to a properly functioning and trustworthy internet. Moving to a model that embraces this is key. Changing how authentication functions and how our models of trust function will be no easy task, but it must be done. Besides, what is wrong with wearing a tinfoil hat when we know the trust model is broken at its foundation, monitoring is ubiquitous and our governments have no real oversight when it comes to technology?

Hactivists Anonymous

"...Anonymity is a shield from the tyranny of the majority... to protect unpopular individuals from retaliation... at the hand of an intolerant society." - McIntyre v. Ohio Elections Commission (1995)

Activism and democracy go hand in hand. The hard-fought accomplishments for equality and justice were paved by those brave enough to question the status quo.

Hactivists are those in the hacker community that have turned toward political activism. This group of people typically fight for the core rights of all humans in an attempt to ensure liberty and justice for all.

One of the most powerful tools used by hactivists is the veil of anonymity.

Anonymity gives every denizen the power to unrestricted self expression. It is a rejection of the surveillance society. It is the ultimate manifestation of freedom of speech, freedom of movement and freedom to associate.

Any system that forbids true anonymity also forbids true freedom.

Where's My Data?

(it isn't here.)

Life in the Walled Garden

We are in an era of walled gardens in the form app stores and eReaders. Access to millions of apps and eBooks are effortlessly at our fingertips. We are promised an amazing experience, secure purchasing and a safe environment. We are offered wonders that do not exist in the outside world.

Walled gardens also represent restriction. They are designed and curated with specific entries and exits. What you experience in the garden stays in the garden after you leave. This is what we call a closed ecosystem.

Disney World is a large walled garden. After paying for a ticket and passing inspection for admittance, Disney World presents you with a tightly controlled experience while in the boundaries of their (very large) walled garden. It is a place of wonder. Everything from food to entertainment have been carefully thought out and curated, every single experience you have within the park has been designed. When you are ready to leave, you exit through the designated exit and you go back to life as usual.

This is the very same model created in software by the Apple App Store, Google Play, Amazon Kindle Store and many others. Each company provides a highly curated, safe and user-friendly experience in exchange for software that is restricted to the specific "walls" of the platform. As long as one lives in the confines of the walled garden, these tools work fantastically well. But if you try to leave the confines of the walled garden, these tools must be left behind.

When you are in the walled garden you have access to tools that are specifically engineered to work there. An iPhone app "feels" like an iPhone app. Kindle Books make reading new books effortless. You can feel confident that the content is safe, that the content has been controlled for quality and that it will work on your device.

The problem with the idea of using the Disney World model for software is that the very people who are protecting you have the potential to abandon you.

The walled garden model assumes several important things. First, it assumes that the garden is relevant. Second, it assumes that the garden's owners are trustworthy.

Walled gardens such as the Apple App Store assume that you not only use an iOS device now, but that you will continue to use an iOS device in the future. Every app that is purchased is non-transferable, meaning once you buy it with your account, you cannot transfer it to a friend or family member later. But, what happens when Apple stops making iOS devices? What happens if Apple goes out of business? This is hard to imagine right now but this very thing has happened time and time again.

We don't have to reach too far into the past to see the predecessor to the App Store, the gaming console. Most gaming consoles are walled gardens. In the 1990s, the Super Nintendo supported Super Nintendo games. They worked exclusively on their hardware and when Nintendo decided to stop developing the console, the walled garden was abandoned. The owners (Nintendo) decided that the platform was no longer relevant.

Walled gardens also assume safety and security. This isn't always the case. Very recently Apple and Google had to deal with apps that made questionable use of smartphone user's personal data. For instance, some developers heavily rely on accessing personal contacts in the phone, as well as geo-location data. Though the overwhelming majority of application developers do not abuse users, there were a small minority of applications that were abusive in nature. This abuse was in the form of sending private information without encryption, selling your behavior to ad networks without your permission, location tracking without permission, and accessing contacts on your phone without your permission. There is almost no oversight on how developers use this collected data. Many are free to sell user data to third parties once they have collected this information.

This isn't to say that we should boycott walled gardens, it's merely to point out that curated experiences that are tightly controlled by a private corporation are appropriate for entertainment and convenience. They are not appropriate for systemic, engineering and foundational function of society, though. We must keep this in mind when we use tools provided to us in a walled garden. It is always appropriate to ask questions like, how will I export my data when this platform is abandoned?

Life in the walled garden isn't reality. It is a curated experience that relies on consumers to fund the operations of the company that owns the walls. As long as the experience seems relevant, the consumers are safe. As soon as a newer and more appealing walled garden pops up down the street, the walled garden risks abandonment and the consumers are left in the dust.

A CLOUD REVOLUTION MANIFESTO

PART 6: OPEN ACCESS

Cassette Tapes and Floppy Disks

The cassette tape was revolutionary. It was easy to use, portable, cheap, tough and compact. But more importantly, people understood how to use it. It was easy to record, copy and share. This empowered people to easily make custom mixed tapes as well as self-publish albums, audiobooks and more. It democratized distribution. All of a sudden a local band could record their own albums and sell tapes at shows. If you were trying to woo someone you could create a one-of-a-kind mixed tape just for that person. And, for the first time, people could easily record their favorite songs on the radio or from vinyl to enjoy while on the go.

When the personal computer revolution started back in the late 1970s, cassette tapes were the obvious choice for storing data. People had tapes. People understood tapes. People loved tapes. Sure, tapes were slow and didn't hold much information, but there was no learning curve and they were cheap. The low-cost cassette tapes, the very same ones you could listen to in your Walkman, could hold computer code. Much like mixtapes, you could now take this code with you and share information with anyone.

Once the idea existed we quickly shifted to media that was faster, cheaper and more reliable. New technology seems to inspire an innovation snowball. For example, the tape led the way the for the floppy disk, the floppy disk led way for the CD-R... and on and on the shift occurs until eventually our personal storage and sharing tools have become mostly cloud-based. These days we just as readily share images, files and music instantly in the cloud.

Sharing is now instant. The medium is invisible. But what the cassette tape inspired hasn't changed.

As humans, our desire to share and self-express are only limited by the technology available to us at the time. As we continue on the path to increasing connectivity, access to information and global communities, our ability to self express and influence one another just gets stronger with time.

Cookbooks and Quilting Clubs

Think about your favorite recipe. How did you come across it? Did you find it in a book? Was it was passed down through your family? Maybe it's a bad photocopy of a recipe your best friend found and it's covered in notes, highlights, modifications and the stains that inevitably come from repeated use next to a sizzling delicacy.

Recipes are meant to be shared, and the best recipes are loved and passed on. In fact, sharing is so ingrained into who we are as humans that advanced sharing cultures have probably been around since before recorded history.

Sure, I can point to hunter-gatherer communities that shared resources, skills and stories for the survival of the tribe, but I am more interested in exploring modern sharing communities.

Notably, there are communities in which the information sharing is central to the health and success of the group as a whole. These communities are groups of people more modernly referred to as Makers.

Makers build things, and most Makers like to share how they build them. This is because maker communities don't base their value on scarcity of information or ownership of information but on the ability of its members to create. Thus the success of the maker group as a whole is the measurement for the success of the individuals in the group.

Let's pretend that you had an elderly relative, let's call her Great-Aunt Bessy, who was part of a quilting club. She happens to be a master quilt maker, one of the best in the state. She also happens to live in a community with an amazing quilting club. Every week, the members would meet to continue work on a group quilting project. They would share techniques and methods in quilting. If someone in the group hadn't mastered a particular skill, someone else in the group would help that person out. The quilting club was amazing due to the fact that it shared knowledge and it cultivated self-betterment. As each individual in the group became more experienced and more capable, the value of the group as a whole increased.

Great-Aunt Bessy was a Maker.

In this way, Great-Aunt Bessy's quilting club and modern day computer and hardware hackers have a lot more in common than you might have previously assumed. This is quite apparent to those of us inspired by the free software movement; a movement that defends and cultivates the free flow of information on computers and the internet. Again, think back on your favorite recipe. Have you ever shared it with anyone? I would venture to guess that you have. Why? Was it because it made particularly good food? Or maybe it was easy? Fast? Cost effective? Maybe it had a license that allowed you to do so?... wait. Did I just say license?

You see, we don't think about "licensing" recipes because the method of cooking, ingredients available, tools used and skill level of the cook all decide the outcome of the food. Overall, more effective recipes are passed on, modified and refined. The best ones get published and ripped out of books, taught in classes and cooked in restaurants. It is never the recipe that is charged for but the outcome of the recipe.

The same is true in quilting clubs.

Quilting is complex, it is social and the outcome is a tangible item that has value. It is gifted or sold and typically contains some sort of deeper meaning. And yet, the reason communities work are not that we charge for quilting methods, quilting patterns, or quilting techniques, but that these communities cultivate the free sharing of techniques and methods.

In writing recipes or quilting, to copy isn't to steal. This is a very important concept in sharing communities. In a sharing community the more people that understand a concept or possess a skill, the more valuable the community is as a whole. When everyone in a community understands something it builds a platform for innovation and new ideas to emerge. Sharing communities, in the end, have the utmost respect for the individual in this way. Sharing communities believe that anyone, with enough ability and drive, should have access to building on one's knowledge to become more capable at whatever that person sets their mind to.

The internet is the world's largest platform for sharing communities. Sharing is the DNA of the internet and innovation is cultivated through sharing communities. The software that powers the world's largest social media websites and the world's most powerful search engine isn't built on licensed code, it is built on open source software. In physics, CERN's super powerful particle accelerators and detectors are reshaping our understanding of the universe. And these instruments could only be built on Linux, a free computer software that was built on a foundation of sharing communities.

Sharing isn't the problem. The problem arises when those who profit from scarcity in the physical world (music, film and publishing industries) try to build artificial barriers and artificial scarcity online. The internet is a brave new world. Instead of attempting to impose 20th century business models for innovation onto 21st century technology, we should look at Great-Aunt Bessy and her world-class quilting club to help us design business models that cultivate innovation for the future.

Big Business Owns Your Thoughts

Imagine a system where individuals contribute to a great work of knowledge. Imagine everyone sharing information and ideas for the good of mankind.

Take Wikipedia for instance, people from all walks of life have helped to build an invaluable, free and open work of knowledge for the benefit of the whole planet. Unfortunately for some among us, they don't see how these types of systems benefit the world. Instead, they see a different system. They see a world where wealth is created only through ownership.

They see a patent system. Where instead of sharing ideas, large corporations and other nefarious entities can buy ideas. They then wield these patents like weapons against individuals and companies that actually create and innovate. They exploit and abuse a poorly designed patent system to destroy competition through pointless litigation.

There is already a system that has an enormous ability to promote growth, innovation and progress. That system is called open access, and it has been applied to fields as diverse as software, solar photovoltaic technology and drug discovery.

It is a system where a group of peers collaborate and barter to create an end product available to the community at no cost; a system where everyone can benefit and prosper.

For example, the Open Source Drug Discovery organization aims to provide a platform for drug researchers to collaborate on finding inexpensive drugs to improve healthcare in the emerging world. By opening research projects to external contributors their research capacity can be significantly increased. Contrast this with the millions of deaths in Africa each year due to infectious diseases that could be prevented if drug companies didn't have drug patents that allow them to block competitors from making the same life-saving drugs cheaper.

The current patent system is a backward and broken system, and it needs to be fixed. The free flow of information should not be impeded by greed and malevolence.

Give it Away

One of the most powerful forces behind the web today is a simple idea that has been around since the dawn of civilization.

If you want to establish an idea as important, if you want to establish thought leadership, if you want others to adopt your way of thinking:

Express yourself clearly and give it away.

The Pirates are coming

The pirates are coming, sailing the open seas of the internet in search of information to consume without permission.

The pirates are coming, copying digital riches and hoarding information in virtual treasure chests.

Though it might be hard for some to digest, pirates are important.

They are the swashbucklers and merry anarchists of the twenty-first century.

They help us question our assumptions on fairness.

They combat the legalistic trap that is modern copyright law.

They challenge us to find new ways to compensate creators without requiring law enforcement and teams of attorneys to be involved.

The pirates are coming, innovating sharing technology, anonymity tools and challenging the status quo.

The pirates are coming, and we should take notes.

On the Shoulders of Giants

"If I have seen further it is by standing on the shoulders of giants." - Sir Isaac Newton

"I had hoisted myself up on the shoulders of giants." - Linus Torvalds

You have probably heard of a man named Sir Isaac Newton. His contributions to physics and mathematics catapulted our civilization's foundational understanding of the universe to dizzying heights. His ideas are taught in high schools and universities to this day. He was also the first to admit that his contributions to humanity were built on a foundation of thoughts and innovation from the "giants" that came before him.

This is the amazing thing about great thinkers like Newton. He happened to be born in the right place at the right time. He happened to have a life that introduced him to ideas about gravity, light, sound and abstract mathematical models. He happened to look at the same world that is around all of his contemporaries, with the same information available to others. And, with all of that, he was able to look at the universe a little bit differently than everyone else. He was able to ask the right questions and build the proper models to test those questions in a way that fundamentally shifted the thinking of all physicists and mathematicians that would come after him.

A name that you may or may not have heard of is Linus Torvalds, the father of Linux. Linux is a free and open source operating system. It is an alternative to operating systems like Apple's Mac OS X and Microsoft's Windows. Linux can be downloaded for free and installed on almost any modern computer hardware, large or small. Linux technology powers everything from Google's Android smartphones to CERN's Large Hadron Collider, the world's largest and most powerful particle accelerator and collider ever built. Linux is the foundational technology that powers Google, Facebook, Amazon and thousands of other engineering-focused web technologies.

What makes Linux special is that, because it is free and open source, it belongs to all of us. It serves as a foundational technology for innovation. It was also built on a wealth of technology that came before it. Linux is part of an academic school of thought that puts this acknowledgment front and center. It is built on the notion that great things are built on clear understanding, peer review and collaboration.

Foundational thinkers like Newton and Torvalds shift our focus and understanding just enough to act as catalysts for innovation and disruption. Their contributions, and the contributions built on top of their ideas, continue to push the boundaries of human understanding.

Everyone on this earth reaps the rewards of the giants of our past. But only with clarity of thought, innovative thinking and the courage to push the boundaries of understanding, are individuals capable of standing on the shoulders of giants. Our future is defined not only by the radically creative thinking, but on whose shoulders you build your thoughts.

Google and the Common Good

The common good is a concept that represents shared knowledge and other resources that benefit society as a whole. A central authority doesn't control the common good and it isn't owned by anyone specifically. The -isms of the 19th and 20th century (capitalism, socialism, communism, etc) were all interested in building systems that served in maximizing the common good (some more successfully than others).

The English language (or any language really) belongs to the common good. English isn't owned by anyone. A corporation does not own it. A government doesn't run it. Its existence is shared by all who use it and the benefits of knowing English are evident (you wouldn't be reading this right now if that weren't true).

The common good lays the foundation for all of civilization. Tools like language, mathematics and the scientific process all rest firmly in the common good. Free and open access to these building blocks of society are what create opportunity, inspire new ideas and allow people to learn, grow and solve interesting problems.

The cloud might be the greatest example of taking this idea to its logical conclusion. In computing, the internet and the cloud, the common good lives on in the form of free and open source software (FOSS). FOSS is a type of software that is free to be used by anyone (free as in freedom) and typically free of cost (free as in free pizza). FOSS is protected by the public domain and anyone is free to distribute, modify and use this code.

Open source software is the lifeblood of the cloud. It helps us build a foundation of code that is reliable, trustworthy and agreed upon. Think of open source software as the infrastructure and building blocks that allow us to build everything on the internet today.

Companies like Google wouldn't be alive today if it weren't for free and open source software. It powers their servers, databases, web applications and much more. It is in the fabric of the company to use and contribute to open source code. This is a value system shared by many of the innovators of the 21st century. Almost everything you touch in the cloud these days owes tremendous gratitude to free and open source software.

But it doesn't stop there. Google doesn't only use free and open source software, they also contribute. To date, Google has contributed over 20 million lines of code to over 900 open source projects. They host over 250,000 open source projects on their servers. They even hold a huge Summer of Code event each year, dedicated to free and open source software.

Free and open source software is so ingrained in companies like Google that they spend a tremendous amount of time giving back. They understand that when computing is founded in the common good it not only benefits Google but the internet-using community as a whole.

This is the attitude of the best-in-breed modern for-profit cloud-focused companies. These companies are confident enough in their skills, and thankful enough in the common good software that they rely on every day, that they take time to give back to the vast amount of shared knowledge that powers the cloud.

PART 7: MOBILE

The Invisible Smart Phone

"Any sufficiently advanced technology is indistinguishable from magic." - Arthur C. Clarke, #3 -Clarke's Three Laws

Electricity is magical.

It powers all of modern human civilization and yet it is practically invisible to you and me. It is there when we need it. We spend zero time thinking about it. For the most part, it just works. Yet, electricity has never been more complex in how it's supplied to all of us. Electric companies and governments are facing more challenging engineering problems than ever before. The problems involving generation, delivery, redundancy, security and consistency only get more complex as the expectations of the population and the user base increase.

And yet, it is virtually invisible to you and me. It is safer, more reliable and more predictable than any other time in our lives.

It wasn't always that way. Early adopters of electricity faced real challenges. Electricity was far from invisible. Some companies in the early 20th century understood the potential of electricity and started using it. This required generators, expensive wiring and teams of electrical experts to be hired by the company full time. These companies actually hired full time electricians to be on staff. These employees would configure and modify the electricity. They would adjust the amperage, voltage and much more.

Electricity was dangerous. There were no modern standards so each business ran things slightly different.

Over time this changed. Electrical standards were established. Safety standards were established. Eventually, the reliability of systems became so streamlined that the full-time electrician on staff became unnecessary.

This brings us back to today where electricity is virtually invisible to the average business.

We see correlation between evolution of the personal computer (and eventually the smartphone) and the evolution of electricity.

Since the 1980s, as they started to embrace the computer, companies began hiring full-time IT professionals. Computers were very complex. There were few standards that were adhered to, so IT staff had to configure and modify the IT infrastructure on their own. Each company ran its own file servers, databases, email servers and more.

But in the 1990s things began to change. The internet was introduced to businesses and quickly started adapting to an "always connected" world.

Businesses also started the evolutionary process of asking the question, "Should we continue to do things as we are now or is there a better way to solve this problem?"

Over time, as the internet got faster, cloud providers got better, and ideas were shared, the internet of things was born.

It became conceivable to run a business that embraces the most cutting edge technology without a single IT professional on staff.

It became possible to run the day to day operations of your company from a mobile device. With the internet as the backbone, PCs birthed smart phones. Now we are in a race to make the smart phone faster, smaller, sleeker and more intuitive.

We are in a race to make the smart phone magical. We are in a race to make the smart phone invisible.

A Couple Billion Asians can't be Wrong

Asia is developing internet users an astonishing rate. For many people in Asia, the experience online is exclusively through mobile devices.

What is astonishing about this trend is that our attitude for mobile websites and mobile apps are largely a "me too" attitude. We build a website to be displayed on a computer and then worry about making a mobile version later.

This is completely backward for a majority of modern web users. The mobile web is perfectly poised for late-adopters to the web. The devices are cheap, portable and use very little energy.

This realization has ushered in the "mobile first" philosophy. This philosophy states that most new users to the internet primarily interact with the world online with their smartphones. What started as a nice to have luxury item in the US has quickly become the primary portal for hundreds of millions of web users.

Your Phone is Smarter than You

You are smart, you work hard, you read books. But there is this little device in your pocket that might be smarter than you!

It knows your habits, it knows where you've been. Every phone call you make can be recorded and saved, every location you travel to can be stored and analyzed. Powerful computers in huge data centers the size of football fields run sophisticated algorithms to determine exactly what they think you want and then sync up with your smart phone to complete the out of body experience.

For some, this augmentation of one's own reality might seem like a crutch. You can easily find the closest restaurant or shop. You can also look up that bit of trivia that you have been arguing about with a friend. But does it mean that we are becoming lazy and dependent on that little device in our pocket?

What happens when you have more than one device on you, maybe a smart watch or Google Glass? Will we lose a bit of ourselves to the collective experience of the masses? Are we becoming just a piece of noise at the end of our devices?

It comes down to perspective, but it also comes down to a new way of experiencing our world. A world that is no longer bound to our localized sphere of influence. We can go global. It's true that our device may be smarter than we are, but it's still our device, which means it does what we tell it to and we can control the experience if we choose.

PART 8: FAILURE

Chaos Monkey

There is a monkey in the cloud. Its name is Chaos Monkey and he is making a mess out of everything he touches.

This isn't a work of fiction. Chaos Monkey is real software. It is designed to create havoc in the cloud. It is a special application that climbs through the cloud while randomly killing servers.

This sounds like a dangerous virus written by hackers, but it isn't. This is an application written by Netflix, the online video streaming service. They unleash Chaos Monkey onto the Netflix cloud to test how resilient they are to failure.

Netflix designs for failure. They understand that failures in any system are inevitable and they use tools like Chaos Monkey for resiliency testing. The logic behind purposefully destroying parts of their own cloud is to ensure that its staff knows how to plan for and deal with failure. Instead of waiting around for a failure to occur, they instigate failures and build software that deals with failures efficiently.

As it says on the Chaos Monkey wiki, "If your application can't tolerate a system failure would you rather find out by being paged at 3 a.m. or after you are in the office having already had your morning coffee?"

Designing a system to predict failure is only half the battle. Testing your predictions on a regular basis is the only way to ensure resiliency. I will take my coffee black and leave some space for a little chaos.

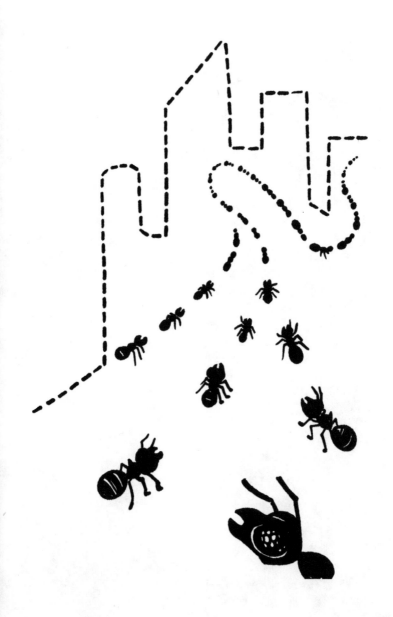

Ants and the Ephemeral Empire

A single red harvester ant colony can last up to twenty years. It sustains and supports more than 10,000 worker ants after only five years of operation. Yet, there is a seeming paradox: This insect empire is built on the fragile, unreliable and short-lived worker ant. These ants don't take orders from a central authority, they are mistake prone and they live only a short period of time (the average worker ant only lives up to one year of age, if it is lucky).

Fortunately, the success of the ant colony does not rest on the shoulders of any single ant. Instead of relying on any one ant to get a job done, the success of the colony is distributed among a large group of ants. In fact, it is the ephemeral nature of the worker ant that forces the ant colony to build on redundancy and resilience. What one ant might not be able to accomplish on its own can easily be accomplished by 1,000 somewhat capable worker ants (with thousands more waiting in the colony below).

This is how the cloud is built. We never think of putting too much responsibility on one server (the ant). Instead we distribute the responsibility to a group of servers, knowing full well that any server can fail at any time.

Taking this a step further, the appearance of a queen (despite her name) and worker ants, the colony does not operate on any central authority. Each ant performs its role in a way that benefits the colony, despite the fact that the queen doesn't truly have any control over her subjects at all. By distributing the authority of the colony to the ants as a whole, no single ant controls the fate of the colony. Each ant's specialized role contributes to the success of the colony as a whole.

Design a system that acknowledges the propensity to failure of any single part and you can reduce failure. Decentralize authority and specialize redundant responsibility and you can build an empire.

Planning for Snoozing Air Traffic Controllers

In 2011, the Federal Aviation Administration (FAA) had a big problem on their hands. It had come to light that on multiple occasions night-shift air traffic controllers had fallen asleep on the job. Though no airplanes had crashed, this issue raised serious safety concerns. The primary danger was that some regional air traffic control towers only employed a single controller for the late night shift. If the solitary controller fell asleep, the control tower failed at its primary mission in keeping the skies safe.

Expanding on the parable that a chain is only as strong as its weakest link, if the entire region under the FAA is relying on a single person not falling asleep at night, ever, we have what is known as a single point of failure. A single point of failure is any identifiable point in any system, that if failure occurs, will cause the entire system to fail.

So how do we fix the snoozing air traffic controller issue?

One option would be to ensure staff never sleeps on the job. A combination of rewards, punishments, breaks and proper training could reduce the odds of a controller sleeping on the job. But in large systems, it isn't appropriate to try to build a single super chain link. We aren't looking for an indestructible chain largely due to the illusion of indestructibility. If a system can fail, eventually it will fail. Before the Titanic sank, everyone was convinced that it was unsinkable.

A better option would be simply to hire a second controller. Adding a second person provides redundancy and resilience to the system and greatly reduces the odds that both controllers would be asleep at the same time.

We see this sort of redundancy in all modern cloud services on many different levels. If Netflix relies on video streaming to make money, they will use hundreds of streaming servers to ensure availability. If anyone streaming server fails, no one even notices. This means that even if a streaming server is unreliable (sleeps on the job) it doesn't matter. Netflix can simply replace it with a properly functioning server in seconds. In the cloud, adequate performance by redundant systems trump perfect performance by a single point of failure.

A CLOUD REVOLUTION MANIFESTO

Semen, Salesmen, and Serendipity

Door-to-door salesmen deal with a lot of rejection. When the average salesman knocks on the door of a random house the odds are very low that he will actually make a sale. If a salesman knows that only 1 in 200 households will buy his product, the only way for the salesman to overcome the failure rate is to make up for it in the number of doors on which he knocks. If he wants to make two sales a week, he needs to plan on knocking on 400 doors.

The salesman is limited by one important factor: he can only knock on one door at a time. In technology we call this serial behavior. The salesman has to finish knocking on the first door before he can move on to the next and then the next.

Reproduction is a bit different. Much like the salesman, semen has a high failure rate (ok, semen has a much higher failure rate). Hundreds of millions of sperm are released, but only one sperm, if it is lucky, will actually unite with the egg. Unlike the salesman, the high failure rate of an individual sperm is compensated by the sheer quantity of sperm transported in semen. In technology we call this parallel behavior. The attempt of all sperm to fertilize the egg happens at the same time. Though only one can be successful, the number of attempts ensures its success.

Both salesmen and sperm have high failure rates. In the first example, the salesman makes up for his serial failure rate by increasing the frequency of attempts at success. In the second example, the semen makes up for its parallel failure rate in sheer numbers. Both, when successful, have a big payoff. Both rely on a mix of opportunity, luck and skill to reach success.

In the cloud, we have the opportunity for both forms of high failure systems. How we design for success depends on how we deal with failure.

PART 9: CONCLUSION

The Santa Claus Hypothesis

To a small child, Santa Claus is very real. Her parents tell her that he is real. Her best friends believe in him. All of her favorite cartoons tell fantastic stories about him. And, sure enough, on Christmas day presents from jolly old Saint Nick are perfectly wrapped and waiting for her under the tree.

Santa is real and he will bring you gifts. Gifts are delivered, therefore, Santa must be real.

Eventually, for all of us, Santa stops being real. Some of us never believed in him. Some of us were told the truth by a friend or a sibling. Some of us figured it out on our own.

As a small child, those of us who believed in Santa were very excited about the proposition of getting awesome gifts from the world's most giving guy. I am sure this is the motivation for many parents to perpetuate the Santa story. They want to give their children the Santa experience, even if it's a lie.

But how many things in life are built around this premise? How many people who have more experience, more understanding or more access to information perpetuate stories to give the rest of us a false narrative to cultivate a specific outcome?

This is one pitfall in the existing cloud movement. As systems become more complex and the knowledge in how these systems function escape the common cloud users, we open the door for false narratives built on the outcomes that we want see and believe.

This is precisely the type of information asymmetry and wish-thinking that we must fight as embracers of disruption and cloud revolutionaries.

To my fellow revolutionaries, I will leave you with this:

Embracing disruption is the act of embracing the unknown. It's the act of letting go of preconceived notions and assumptions of how things must work in favor of testing assumptions of how things could and should work. Embracing disruption is opening one's mind to accepting rapid changes and improvements in thinking and structures.

Rapid changes in thinking alone won't get us far. It can only work if these changes are backed by reliable information and measurable improvements. Those who are successful at embracing disruption are armed with the imagination of an artist, the reasoning of a philosopher and the tools of a scientist.

Our entire model of the universe is based on assumptions. And, for the most part, assumptions get us through life until they stop serving us well. When we run into problems it typically stems from assumptions we made that turned out to be incompatible with reality.

When we speak of embracing disruption we aren't simply speaking of the cloud; we are speaking of embracing disruptions in all aspects of our lives. This includes questioning assumptions in faith, government, economics, equality, justice, sustainability and anything else that suffers from an asymmetry in information and perspective in the world around us.

We advocate a data-driven existence. We advocate building systems that do not rely on central authorities, that aren't too big to fail, and that empower all humans with solid ideas and a fresh way of looking at things to express themselves.

To us, the cloud represents the ultimate playground for the mind.

The cloud isn't governed by the power of your family, what schools you attend or how much money you make. The cloud is governed by the quality of your ideas and your ability to express yourself clearly.

Information is the lifeblood of the cloud. Free movement of information is key. The cloud doesn't tolerate censorship. It has been said that when expression is censored the internet considers it an error and routes around the censurer. The cloud represents the free movement of information and the platform for the free expression of ideas.

We are in the midst of radical shift in how we are structured as a civilization.

We know that no one can predict the future and we embrace that.

We know that replication, modification and distribution are the foundations of life.

We are doers and builders and dreamers.

Some say the term "cloud" is too ambiguous and that disruption is too frightening.

We reject these notions.
The cloud isn't a sales pitch.
It isn't a fad.
It isn't a buzzword.
The cloud has substance.
Disruption has significance.
We are the embracers of disruption.
This is our cloud revolution manifesto.

Epilogue

We really appreciate you reading our manifesto. Help us continue the conversation.

Go to: http://embracingdisruption.com

You can sign up for our newsletter, subscribe to our weekly podcast and find news about ongoing projects.